Joyful Women in a Sorrowful World

Strength in Sacrificial Love

Lectio Divina Meditations

Kathy Pardue

United States Copyright Office
Registration Number TXu2-305-164
Effective Date: February 19, 2022

Dedicated to Lee, Hannah, Juliet and their many joyful olive shoots.

Table of Contents

Preface

I hope to inspire women to find strength in the joyful heart of God in our sorrowful world of uncertainty and chaos. Jesus' offer to infuse us with his full joy is a message we need now to live above the line of despair. Writing during a pandemic and world conflict, I see women seeking hope through a new church, ideology, leader, relationship, or spirituality. The call to sacrificial love is the only path to this sustaining joy, and I encourage women to hear and act on his words to abide in his love and love others. Mary's words are relevant now and always.

> His mother said to the servants, "Do whatever he tells you." [1]

Knowing Jesus endured agony, rejection, and death by the presence of joy captures my heart and motivates these meditations. This book is also written primarily for those who see God's living Word as their authority. If not, scriptures are gathered here to consider in your own search for hope, joy, and strength.

I envision women becoming a powerful support for the hopeless, especially the children. Hope is emphasized because he has spoken loudly to our needs as women through the Incarnation, and these scriptures offer a deep intimacy with our Blessed Hope.

> Thy words were found, and I ate them, and thy words
> became to me a joy and the delight of my heart; [2]

In Lectio Divina, or sacred reading, we simply read (lectio), meditate (meditatio), pray from the heart (oratio), and contemplate (union). There is no striving, only desire, grace, and love.

The beautiful saints mentioned here found joy in the Pearl of Great Value as they persevered to the end. As a counselor and grandmother, I also feel like St. Teresa of Avila attempting anything to help, "But what do I know. I'm just a wretched woman." I encourage women to form groups to read, pray, and act inspired by St. Catherine of Siena. The bella brigata, beautiful circle of friends, was their strong support during the Black Plague. We *will* scatter as lights fixed on him above political or eschatological narratives because he is above it all. I pray his holy joy spreads like the fire of his love! We can be not afraid.

The joy mingled with sorrow will always be available through the discovery of the Pearl, our journey, intimacy with God, and his virtues forming in us. As women who accept and carry out his will as our own, we can see that he has truly been with us. "I have been crucified with Christ; it is no longer I who live, but Christ who lives in me; and the life I now live in the flesh I live by faith in the Son of God, who loved me and gave himself for me." [3]

1   John 2:5
2   Jeremiah 15:16.
3   Galatians 2:20

Introduction

These things I have spoken to you, that my joy may be in you,
and that your joy may be full. [1]

In his compassion, Jesus spoke about giving us his joyful, eternal perspective for our journey so that our days are filled with peace and free from anxiety. How is it possible to live in his state of full joy in our modern world?

The secret to holy joy is responding to *these things* he repeated in John 15. What are they? It is about what we ***do***. *Abiding* in his love and *loving people* are inseparable paths to real joy. Not perfectly, and always by his grace, but he sees our intent to live *in* his love. Any other path is a temporary and self-serving lifestyle for feeling better emotionally. What Jesus means by his love is more than affection, comfort, romance, sentiment, or warm attachments. He went around doing good out of sacrificial love, and we become lights of his Incarnation when we imitate his lifestyle of love.

Finding the Pearl of Great Value releases deep joy helping us let go of inferior pearls. Faith, hope, and love are virtues *deposited* in us as more virtues grow *through our suffering.* We long to see Jesus face to face but resist the mingling of joy and sorrow on our journey. It was joy beyond the sorrow which helped Jesus endure the cross and despise the shame. Fearless martyrs looked toward being with him, and some even ran to their death. This sounds unrealistic until we have his grace at the hour of our death.

God understands our fleshly fears and comforts us with Jesus' own response in his humanity. In the days of his flesh, Jesus offered up prayers and supplications, with loud cries and tears, to him who was able to save him from death, and he was heard for his godly fear. [2]

Our Blessed Mother expressed her joy in the Magnificat, yet she experienced seven sorrows knowing a sword would pierce her heart over her son's sufferings and death. Helpless to help, his pain as her own, and deep sadness as he laid in her arms were Mary's sorrows. The infusion of joy is a real process giving us strength in fatigue, sickness, betrayal, trauma, and death. His joy in us is an invisible condition giving interior strength. We consume your words in prayer. Infuse us with your joy, O Lord.

1   John 15:11
2   Hebrews 5:7

Joy of the Pearl

Sustainer

But thou, O LORD, art a shield about me, my glory,
and the lifter of my head. I cry aloud to the LORD,
and he answers me from his holy hill. I lie down and
sleep. I wake again, for the LORD sustains me. [1]

We can enter a deep rest in a world of unrest because the Lifter of our head shields and answers us. He is the *real* reality and fully able to strengthen us during instability. When we cannot see his answers or feel his presence, he is still Emmanuel, God with us. He is good and fully able! For they are thy people and thy heritage, whom thou didst bring out by thy great power and by thy outstretched arm. [2]

The best world news today is the kingdom of the Ancient of Days will *not* be destroyed! I saw in the night visions, and behold, with the clouds of heaven there came one like a son of man, and he came to the Ancient of Days and was presented before him. And to him was given dominion and glory and kingdom, that all peoples, nations, and languages should serve him; his dominion is an everlasting dominion, which shall not pass away, and his kingdom one that shall not be destroyed. [3]

God is not concerned with time or panicked from the unfolding of events. Is he able to sustain us in the threat of famine, fires, floods, population, tsusamis, viruses, and war in addition to our daily concerns? Yes, and there is no greater security and source of information to comfort and direct us than the eternal Word of Christ. His ways of sustaining the world are beyond our understanding. For my thoughts are not your thoughts, neither are your ways my ways, says the Lord. [4] Most things are beyond our control, but the Lord is fully aware and is not indifferent or worried about time.

My times are in thy hand; deliver me from the hand of my enemies and persecutors! [5] I lift up my eyes to the hills. From whence does my help come?

My help comes from the LORD, who made heaven and earth. The LORD is your keeper; the LORD is your shade on your right hand. The LORD will keep your going out and your coming in from this time forth and for evermore. [6]

1   Psalm 3:3-5
2   Deuteronomy 9:29
3   Daniel 7:13.14
4   Isaiah 55:8
5   Psalm 31:15
6   Psalm 121:1,2,5,8

My reflections.
Lectio, reading the Scripture...slowly

Meditation, drawn to these words...

Prayer of the heart...

Contemplation...silence

Spoken

Sanctify them in the truth; thy word is truth. [1]

Jesus spoke this about his Living Word. *Why* can we trust his spoken words? Our confidence in his words comes from his relationship with God, inspiration of Sacred Scripture, Sacred Tradition, and faith. Now they know that everything that thou hast given me is from thee; for I have given them the words which thou gavest me, and they have received them and know in truth that I came from thee; and they have believed that thou didst send me. [2]

We can trust *Sacred Scripture* preserved for us. All scripture is inspired by God and profitable for teaching, for reproof, for correction, and for training in righteousness, [3] Go therefore and make disciples of all nations, baptizing them in the name of the Father and of the Son and of the Holy Spirit, teaching them to observe all that I have commanded you; and lo, I am with you always, to the close of the age. [4]

We can trust *Sacred Tradition* handed down by *word of mouth* or by *letter.*
So then, brethren, stand firm and hold to the traditions which you
were taught by us, either by word of mouth or by letter. [5]
I commend you because you remember me in everything and maintain
the traditions even as I have delivered them to you. [6]
And they devoted themselves to the apostles' teaching and fellowship,
to the breaking of bread and the prayers. [7]

The *Deposit of Faith* includes **all** teachings preserved which were
written or oral. [8] Tradition serves Sacred Scripture.
He who hears you hears me, and he who rejects you rejects
me, and he who rejects me rejects him who sent me. [9]

The *Church* protects and preserves the teachings of Christ.
if I am delayed, you may know how one ought to behave in the household of God,
which is the church of the living God, the pillar and bulward of the truth. [10]

We are *protected* from private interpretations with no authority.
First of all you must understand this, that no prophecy of
scripture is a matter of one's own interpretation, [11]

1	John 17:17
2	John 17:7,8
3	II Timothy 3:16
4	Matthew 28:19,20
5	2 Thess. 2:15
6	I Cor. 11:2.
7	Acts 2:42
8	CCC 85,86
9	Luke 10:16
10	I Timothy 3:15
11	I Peter 1:20

My reflections.
Lectio, reading the Scripture...slowly

Meditation, drawn to these words...

Prayer of the heart...

Contemplation...silence

Infusion

As the Father has loved me, so I have loved you; abide in my love.
These things I have spoken to you, that my joy may be in you,
and that your joy may be full. This is my commandment,
that you love one another as I have loved you. [1]

What are "these things" he has spoken so that his joy may be in us? His holy joy is infused in us when we abide in his love and love people. He knows the intent in our hearts to try even when we fail to love in our thoughts and in our words. We have free will to be indifferent, do mediocre love, or intentionally abide in him.

To not abide detaches me from myself and others. My soul suffers if I ignore his whisper to be silent in exchange for productivity, and others suffer if I neglect duties. While we sit with him like Mary who chose the best, we can also serve like Martha in interior worship as he orders our steps. St. Catherine worshiped at the kitchen sink sometimes in ecstasy as she served a large family.

Why does Jesus offer an infusion of his joy? It was his great *compassion* for our journey he spoke *so that* we can live in the strength of *his* joy! We are prone to fear and need divine joy in chaos. The world needs our comfort, especially the children. Edith Stein said, "The world doesn't need what women have, it needs what women are. The woman's soul is fashioned as a shelter in which other souls may unfold." Edith was a philosophy professor, martyr, and saint who taught on the boldness of women before she died at Auschwitz.

Joy flows from the love. To know you are loved by even one person has a stabilizing affect during intense suffering. In doing group therapy for adolescents and young adults in a hospital, I saw those with suicidal ideation felt no one loved them. When I asked if I could be hope for them, they responded in doubt, then tears. In the children's wing, they just wanted to go home with me. There is a reality behind his words that love never fails!

Many waters cannot quench love, neither can floods drown it. If a man offered for love all the wealth of his house, it would be utterly scorned. [2]

1   John 15:9, 11, 12
2   Song of Solomon 8:7

My reflections.
Lectio, reading the Scripture...slowly

Meditation, drawn to these words...

Prayer of the heart...

Contemplation...silence

Joy

For this day is holy to our Lord; and do not be grieved,
for the joy of the Lord is your strength. [1]

What is it? *Joy* is a constant, sustaining condition. Unlike happiness, joy has no visible signs of pleasure. Joyful women have an inner spark helping them interpret life through a lens of hope and strength beyond resilience. *Happiness*, according to St. Thomas Aquinas, is the contemplation of truth sought for its own sake and is the perfection and well-being of our souls which we can never fully achieve in this life. [2]

Real joy is not related to mood, age, culture, education, race, or temperament. Life is not easier for these women, but they genuinely listen and offer a smile during their own suffering.

In some seasons, crying may be every day. Joy is not denial of pain or a false persona. Space is reserved for lightheartedness, and they receive forgiveness with gratitude knowing their desperate need for grace and mercy. No time for scrupulosity, false guilt, or legalism for these women who see time as opportunity to create beauty, relationship, and work for the common good. Each day has enough trouble of its own to doubt God's goodness or clutter the soul with drama from questionable friends or false accusations. We are made for his good pleasure.

Thou dost show me the path of life; in thy presence there is fulness of joy,
in thy right hand are pleasures forevermore. [3]

A joyful therapist near retirement often slid comments under my door at 7am. She decided to encourage me knowing the intensity of couples counseling and our dependency on God to help. She knew fear of death underlies anxiety and wrote, "By the way, never worry about dying; he'll be right there with you." St. Catherine of Siena said, "Never worry about death, it's the easiest thing to do." This is not to minimize our pain and suffering, but a reminder of the beatific vision of God waiting for us where joy and love will be billions of lightyears beyond our comprehension.

1   Nehemiah 8:10b
2   Summa Contra Gentiles, book 3, chapter 37
3   Psalm 16:11

My reflections.
Lectio, reading the Scripture...slowly

Meditation, drawn to these words...

Prayer of the heart...

Contemplation...silence

Pearl

*Again, the kingdom of heaven is like a merchant in search of fine pearls, who,
on finding one pearl of great value, went and sold all that he had and bought it.* [1]

Women search for valuable pearls in the beautiful, helpful, intellectual, meaningful, memorable, pleasurable, purposeful, and relational. We are complicated and gifted! Finding the *most* valuable pearl, Jesus, produces great joy.
Without having seen him you love him; though you do not now see him
you believe in him and rejoice with unutterable and exalted joy. [2]

When we intentionally seek and find him, other pursuits lose priority. When other pearls compete and lure us to replace him, we suffer and feel the loss. If we find him casually in a field, we may drift and see him over time. He has surprising, creative ways of pursuing us as the Lover of our Souls.

The pearl is formed over a long period of time through the oyster's suffering to produce perfect beauty. An oyster secretes a chemical forming around a grain of sand or irritant forming layers of mother-of-pearl. Jesus' willing sacrifice of himself for us reconciled us to God,
For to us a child is born, to us a son is given; and the government
will be upon his shoulder, and his name will be called "Wonderful
Counselor, Mighty God, Everlasting Father, Prince of Peace." [3]
In his humanity, Jesus learned through suffering.
Although he was a Son, he learned obedience through what he suffered; [4]

Searching for beauty whether in birthing, creating, designing, gathering, learning, nurturing, teaching, or working is how he fashions us for his glory. No failure or suffering is wasted in our formation. The Incarnation captures our heart as we respond to our Bridegroom, and the saints' lives show how suffering formed their love and intimacy with Jesus. Jesus radiates the Father, and we sense his beauty in our souls, creation, Scriptures, Eucharist, and souls of people.

He reflects the glory of God and bares the very stamp of his
nature, upholding the universe by his word of power. [5]

1   Matthew 13:45,46
2   I Peter 1:8
3   Isaiah 9:6
4   Hebrews 5:8
5   Hebrews 1:3a

My reflections.
Lectio, reading the Scripture...slowly

Meditation, drawn to these words...

Prayer of the heart...

Contemplation...silence

Love

Having purified your souls by your obedience to the truth for a sincere love of the brethren, love one another earnestly from the heart. [1]

St. John of the Cross said, "In the evening of life, we will be judged on love alone." St. Teresa of Avila prayed, "The surest sign of my love for you is the degree of perfection with which I keep the commandment of charity toward my neighbor." We fail here.

How much and in what ways does St. Peter mean by *earnestly* love from the heart? Love can be expressed through words, affection, serving, support, and prayer. No temperament is exempt from our call to love. We are encouraged to go beyond tolerating others, and withholding love may be a sign of indifference, resentment, selfishness, or unforgiveness. Earnest love also prays for nations, strangers, enemies, and the lonely who have no one to pray for them. Even in a necessary boundary for safety, love prays for healing and reconciliation. Love does not count offenses or consider a wrong suffered. As Joseph forgave his brothers for selling him into slavery and later saved them from starvation, he showed the sacrificial love of Jesus in horrible betrayal and injustice. God's love knows no limits.

Showing love also means listening for the heart message. Edith Stein said, "Women comprehend not only with the intellect, but also with the heart." Women do not talk simply to exchange data; we want connection. Love is asking questions, being attentive, and investing. Jesus wailed with loud crying and tears when his friend, Lazarus, died. We are made in his image, and framing souls as logical *or* emotional is a false dichotomy. God is passionate about his creation, and the virtues reflect his heart.

His knowledge is *incomprehensible*. Where were you when I laid the foundation of the earth? Tell me if you have understanding. Who determined its measurements—surely you know! Or who stretched the line upon it? On what were its bases sunk, or who laid its cornerstone, when the morning stars sang together, and all the sons of God shouted for joy? [2]

His love is *unfathomable*. What is man that thou art mindful of him, and the son of man that thou dost care for him? [3]

1   Peter 1:22
2   Job 38:4-7
3   Psalm 8:4

My reflections.
Lectio, reading the Scripture...slowly

Meditation, drawn to these words...

Prayer of the heart...

Contemplation...silence

Dance

Thou hast turned for me my mourning into dancing; thou hast loosed my sackcloth and girded me with gladness, that my soul may praise thee and not be silent. O LORD my God, I will give thanks to thee forever. [1]

Gratitude can cause an explosion of joy and movement in women after physical and emotional healing. As we offer up our suffering, we enter his passion and know he is truly near the brokenhearted. Reality shifts when he adjusts our attitude during depression on temporal earthly sufferings not to be compared with his coming glory. Even if our circumstances do not change, our soul cannot be silent and may break out in song and dance celebrating new awareness. He is the restorer of our souls!

Accepting what he allows even unto death is living in his will, and there is a time for weeping and rejoicing. The early church, comprised of Jewish believers, danced in celebration of the Torah and life, just as David danced before the Ark of the Covenant, rejoicing as they returned it to Jerusalem.

A gifted friend choreographed interpretive ballet, jazz, and Israeli dance for her liturgical dance company in response to his beauty. This dance form portrays God's creation and goodness as well as our responses of joy and sorrow in trials. We worshipped as twelve dancers interpreting Genesis' stories of sin, joy, praise, suffering, and redemption. Angels of the four winds, prayer warriors in battle, kyrie eleison, forgiveness, reaping and sowing, what we gave to love, and celebration of love glorified God through dance.

St. Teresa of Avila said, "My God, protect me from gloomy saints." Movement is healing and a beautiful form of praise. He turns our mourning into dancing, and you are free to dance before him.

And the LORD will guide you continually, and satisfy your desire with good things, and make your bones strong; and you shall be like a watered garden, like a spring of water, whose waters fail not. [2]

1   Psalm 30:11-12
2   Isaiah 58:11

My reflections.
Lectio, reading the Scripture...slowly

Meditation, drawn to these words...

Prayer of the heart...

Contemplation...silence

Glory

The heavens are telling the glory of God; and the firmament proclaims his handiwork.
Day to day pours forth speech, and night to night declares knowledge. [1]

To comprehend the Holy One with our finite mind is impossible, yet we are held responsible for a resistant heart. Wisdom admits how little we know, and not to stand in awe at the vastness of our universe and bow in humility is foolish.

Then Moses said, "Now, please show me your glory. The LORD answered,
"I will cause all my goodness to pass in front of you,
and I will announce my name, the LORD, so you can hear it." [2]

We cannot know him without his grace and revelation. Only by grace, humility, and purity of heart can we even come closer.
"Blessed are the pure in heart, for they shall see God." [3]

The majesty of God demands our silence and adoration.

St. Thomas Aquinas received a vision of the Lord during Mass in 1273 which changed his life. "The end of my labor has come. I can write no more. I have seen things that make my writings like straw." He also heard Christ say, "You have written well of me, Thomas." He did not complete the Summa Theologiae and died shortly after. Scholars say this vision of glory was not a retraction of his writings as Doctor of the Church. [4]

We will see the beatific vision of God at the appointed time.
For now we see in a mirror dimly, but then face to face.
Now I know in part; then I shall understand fully,
even as I have been fully understood. [5]

It is hard for those in confusion and anger wandering in endless arguments and philosophies seeking God or defying his existence. The heart longs for our father who knows us intimately. Too many voices, wounding, historical, political evils, and religious wars have led many to trust only self as their authority. Lord, have mercy on us as we wait for your unveiling of Truth.

1   Psalm 19:1-2
2   Exodus 33:19
3   Matthew 5:8
4   www.catholic.com qa when-st-thomas
5   I Cor. 13:12

My reflections.
Lectio, reading the Scripture...slowly

Meditation, drawn to these words...

Prayer of the heart...

Contemplation...silence

Home

But our commonwealth is in heaven, and from it we await a Savior, the Lord Jesus Christ, [1]

We are on our way back home. Do you sense the lack of permanence? Having the same job or living in the same house for thirty years may provide consistency, but events and relationships are changing. We are not home but living as "aliens and exiles" on the earth as we try to live to glorify God through good deeds. [2] Even as we are ridiculed, misunderstood, or hated, we know this earth is passing, and joy awaits in our real home with Abba Father.

Every year has elements of joy, grief, and loss no matter how much we try to create continuity and safety. It may feel so random but is all his plan. Man is like a breath; his days are like a passing shadow. [3]

This is not reason for depression, anxiety, insanity, or suicide because we are loved and not alone. The first scripture I taught my children was about where our real help and safety come from.

Hence we can confidently say, "The Lord is my helper,
I will not be afraid; what can man do to me?" [4]

Thou dost guide me with thy counsel, and afterward thou wilt receive me to glory.
Whom have I in heaven but Thee? And there is nothing upon earth that
I desire besides thee. My flesh and my heart may fail,
but God is the strength of my heart and my portion forever. [5]

For my father and my mother have forsaken me, but the LORD will take me up. [6]

The Catechism clarifies our citizenship is in heaven: Christ's Ascension marks the definitive entrance of Jesus' humanity into God's heavenly domain, whence he will come again (cf. Acts 1:11); this humanity in the meantime hides him from the eyes of men (cf. Col 3:3). Jesus Christ, the head of the Church, precedes us into the Father's glorious kingdom so that we, the members of his Body, may live in the hope of one day being with him forever. Jesus Christ, having entered the sanctuary of heaven once and for all, intercedes constantly for us as the mediator who assures us of the permanent outpouring of the Holy Spirit. [7]

1	Philippians 3:20
2	I Peter 2:11
3	Psalm 144:4
4	Hebrews 13:6
5	Psalm 73:24-26
6	Psalm 27:10
7	CCC 665-667

My reflections.
Lectio, reading the Scripture...slowly

Meditation, drawn to these words...

Prayer of the heart...

Contemplation...silence

Vision

his head and his hair were white as white wool, white as snow;
his eyes were like a flame of fire, his feet were like burnished bronze, refined
as in a furnace, and his voice was like the sound of many waters;
in his right hand he held seven stars, from his mouth issued a sharp two-edged sword,
and his face was like the sun shining in full strength. [1]

The Lord gave visions here to St. John of the Revelation or unveiling. He gave visions to the patriarchs, prophets, apostles, and saints. Visions are given for the future, direction, intimacy, warnings, and glimpses of his glory.

We will see his Name.
And he was clothed with a vesture dipped in blood; and his name is called
The Word of God. [2] And he had on his vesture and on his thigh a name written,
KING OF KINGS, AND LORD OF LORDS.
Even so. Amen. [3]

We will fall in his Holy Presence.
When I saw him, I fell at his feet as though dead. [4]
And the twenty-four elders and the four living creatures fell down and
worshiped God who is seated on the throne, saying "Amen. Hallelujah!" [5]

Beatific Vision
Because of his transcendence, God cannot be seen as he is, unless he himself opens up his mystery to man's immediate contemplation and gives him the capacity for it. The Church calls this contemplation of God in his heavenly glory "the beatific vision." [6]

Pour out your Spirit
The Lord will continue to give visions as he pours out his Spirit on all flesh as time unfolds.

And in the last days it shall be, God, declares, that I will pour out my Spirit upon all flesh, and your sons and our daughters shall prophesy, and your young men shall see visions and your old men shall dream dreams; [7]

1	Revelation 1:14,15
2	Revelation 19:13
3	Revelation 19:16
4	Revelation 1:17
5	Revelation 19:4
6	CCC 1028
7	Acts 2:17

My reflections.
Lectio, reading the Scripture...slowly

Meditation, drawn to these words...

Prayer of the heart...

Contemplation...silence

Joy of the Journey

Purpose

By this my Father is glorified, that you bear much fruit, and so prove to be my disciples.
You did not choose me, but I chose you and appointed you that you should go
and bear fruit and that your fruit should abide; [1]

We were chosen to bear fruit for God's glory. Our life is not our own, and our spiritual gifts and talents are given for others.

So, we are alive for God's purposes! St. Paul said,

For to me to live is Christ, and to die is gain. [2]

Nameless, faceless saints are doing deeds having favor with God we will never know. He reveals our purpose through our gifts and desires as he orders our steps for his good pleasure. He sees the intent of our heart to serve him. We do not need to worry, focus, or obsess on our legacy because it is not about us. He knows whose lives we have touched even briefly. Since our life is a mere breath, but known forever in eternity, we do not need to *fear* being forgotten or not doing enough to be loved by him.

Fear not, for I have redeemed you; I have called you by name, you are mine. [3]

He is our reward. Spiritual ambition and vainglory only bring our reward in full on *earth*. Thus, when you give alms, sound no trumpet before you, as the hypocrites do in the synagogues and in the streets, that they may be praised by men. Truly, I say to you, they have their reward. [4]

Saint Teresa of Calcutta said, "We can't do many great things for God, but we can do many small things with great love." She was not focused on her effectiveness, but on worshiping Jesus through her hands and heart. Truly, truly, I say to you, unless a grain of wheat falls into the earth and dies, it remains alone; but if it dies, it bears much fruit. [5] The saints' stories are full of sorrow over sin, and most consider themselves prone to wickedness in their prayers. Because of their humility in confession, he uses their battles for healing, saving souls, and teaching. Our purpose is discovered without striving and is in sync with his will when we are abandoned to divine providence! We are freed from our obsession with significance. All glory and honor are yours', O Lord.

1   John 15:8, 16
2   Philippians 1:21
3   Isaiah 43:1
4   Matthew 6:2
5   John 12:24

My reflections.
Lectio, reading the Scripture...slowly

Meditation, drawn to these words...

Prayer of the heart...

Contemplation...silence

Sheep

*My sheep hear my voice, and I know them, and they follow me;
and I give them eternal life, and they shall never perish,
and no one shall snatch them out of my hand.* [1]

So, joy infusion happens as we hear and act on his *simple* call to stay in his love and love others? Not so *simple*! We also behave like dumb sheep who are hard of hearing and forgetful. We worry, get angry, and are selfish. We must be baaad. No, we are not bad. If we hear real guilt through the Holy Spirit, that is good, and we are restored by grace in the sacrament of confession. Our hardness of hearing improves over time as we learn to hear his voice, and we are safe with our Good Shepherd. He is watching over us.

In The Interior Castle, St. Teresa of Avila wrote, "Do not think lightly sisters, of this first grace nor be downcast if you have not responded immediately to Our Lord's voice, for His Majesty is willing to wait for us many a day and even many a year, especially when He sees perseverance and good desires in our hearts." [2]

She continued, "beware of the poisonous reptiles—that is to say, the bad thoughts and aridities which are often permitted by God to assail and torment us so that we cannot repel them. Indeed, perchance we feel their sting! He allows this to teach us to be more on our guard in the future and to see whether we grieve much at offending him. Therefore, if you occasionally lapse into sin, do not lose heart and cease trying to advance, for God will draw good even out of our falls. Can any evil be greater than that we find at home? What peace can we hope to find elsewhere if we have none within us? Peace, peace be unto you, my sisters, as our Lord said, and many a time proclaimed to his Apostles." [3]

"They should confide in God's mercy, trusting nothing in themselves; then they will see how His Majesty will lead them from one mansion to another, and will set them in a place where these wild beasts can no more touch or annoy them." [4]

1   John 10:27
2   St. Teresa of Avila, Interior Castle, The Second Mansions, 6.
3   St. Teresa of Avila, Interior Castle, The Second Mansions, 16.
4   St. Teresa of Avila, Interior Castle, The Second Mansions, 17.

My reflections.
Lectio, reading the Scripture...slowly

Meditation, drawn to these words...

Prayer of the heart...

Contemplation...silence

Unity

I in them and thou in me, that they may become perfectly one,
so that the world may know that thou hast sent me and hast loved them,
even as thou hast loved me. [1]

Jesus' prayer was for us to be *perfectly one*. Our fragmented body is not perfectly one, but a unified body is possible because his prayer is still valid in our modern world. This is the Father's heart. His purpose in praying oneness was to show the world God's love for them is *real*. His decrees will happen, and our prayers are heard.

There is *one* body and one Spirit, just as you were called to the one hope that belongs to your call, *one* Lord, *one* faith, *one* baptism, *one* God and Father of us all, who is above all and through all and in all. [2]

We need each other and are on the same team. Christians are showing the love of God *is* real in many joint ministries, and our faith *is* working through love. For in Christ Jesus neither circumcision nor uncircumcision is of any avail, but faith working through love. [3]

We are not *perfectly* one as Jesus prayed, however, but can work toward oneness as we surrender to his prayer in the garden. He will reveal the way as we agree with him things are not yet as he desires. If we avoid quarrels, we are obeying him and spreading the fragrance of Christ even as a fragmented body.

Have nothing to do with stupid, senseless controversies;
you know that they breed quarrels. [4]

Let your kingdom come, O Lord. Make us perfectly one, Father, to show the world you sent Jesus and love them. We can embrace each other through the Holy Spirit and trust him to unite us *even* on Jesus' hard saying.

He who eats my flesh and drinks my blood abides in me, and I in him.
Many of his disciples, when they heard it, said, "This is a hard saying;
who can listen to it?" But Jesus, knowing in himself that his disciples
murmured at it, said to them, "Do you take offense at this? Jesus said
to the twelve, "Will you also go away?" Simon Peter answered him,
"Lord, to whom shall we go? You have the words of eternal life; [5]

1   John 17:23
2   Ephesians 4:4-5
3   Galatians 5:6
4   2 Tim. 2:23
5   John 6:56, 60, 61, 67, 68

My reflections.
Lectio, reading the Scripture...slowly

Meditation, drawn to these words...

Prayer of the heart...

Contemplation...silence

Community

not neglecting to meet together, as is the habit of some,
but all the more as you see the Day drawing near. [1]

Community is part of his plan and even more as time passes. Many women feel isolated and abandoned during the multiple crises happening in our world. Feelings will come, but we can decide to not neglect our meeting together and resist the spirit of the world's drift toward solation, confusion, and despair. We can reach out to be an extension of Jesus' love when things fall apart. He knows our insecurities and is our helper. We will be not afraid.

The lack of trust in leadership, fear of illness, and threats of war have created mass hopelessness. Loneliness is overwhelming and the root cause of many academic, emotional, physical, economic, and family problems. How can we opt out of anger and panic to trust God who is the restorer of broken things? We can fix our minds on Jesus through prayer, study, and serving each other. We have choices. Women can become life-giving hope to others.

We had six feet of water in our house after a hurricane, but the flood, by his grace, did not consume me. I grieved the sudden loss of everything familiar, but he helped me accept the changes and investment in community to enter the next season of my life. He used the trauma for good, again, on my journey. By his grace, I talked on Hope in Despair a few weeks after moving.

By communicating what God has spoken through the prophets and Gospels, we are instruments of healing hearts all around us. We are imitators Christ who *went around doing good.* Having a curious heart is necessary but being an extrovert is not. Encouragement is important for motivation and good mental health. When we see sad or avoidant eyes, a simple question can be like a cup of cold water. Reaching out is hard, especially in depression, but meal sharing and serving shows love and support as extensions of his love.

1   Hebrews 10:25

My reflections.
Lectio, reading the Scripture...slowly

Meditation, drawn to these words...

Prayer of the heart...

Contemplation...silence

Perspective

*looking to Jesus the pioneer and perfecter of our faith, who for the joy
that was set before him endured the cross, despising the shame,
and is seated at the right hand of the throne of God.* [1]

To live in sustaining joy and strength, we need God's mind on the mingling of joyful and sorrowful mysteries of the Rosary. He tells us to be not
afraid, but we feel shame because we *do* believe he is trustworthy, and yet
we fear. He knows we are naturally pain avoidant and sympathizes with our
weaknesses.

In his humanity, Jesus did not fear, fight back, or avoid. His strength
was in trusting his Father who upholds the universe by his word of power.
His joy was constant and invisible, and his lens was clear. Ours', not so much,
because we forget or do not believe his words.

> For now we see in a mirror dimly, but then face to face. Now I know in
> part; then I shall understand fully, even as I have been fully understood. [2]

The effects of world problems and personal suffering, as serious as they
are, are not worthy to be compared to what we will experience when we
see him.

> I consider that the sufferings of this present time are not worth
> comparing with the glory that is to be revealed to us. [3]

Gazing at the Pearl in adoration produces holy joy and peace. Love from
his sacred heart pours into our hearts. Then, love desires to love people.

> Without having seen him you love him; though you do not now see him
> you believe in him and rejoice with unutterable and exalted joy. [4]

As more familiar comforts are threatened or removed, we can be assured
he is all we need. Lord, help us to depend less on externals and know your
dwelling place is inside our spirits. Help us to be content in whatever state we

are in as St. Paul taught. Give us your perspective on joy and sorrow mingled together, O Lord.

1   Hebrews 12:2
2   I Cor 13:12
3   Romans 8:18
4   I Peter 1:8

My reflections.
Lectio, reading the Scripture...slowly

Meditation, drawn to these words...

Prayer of the heart...

Contemplation...silence

Freedom

and you will know the truth, and the truth will make you free. [1]

Joyful women love truth. Jesus is the Truth, and all truth comes from God. We see individuals and groups express truth on all sides of issues knowing there is gray, and there is black and white. At the unveiling, or revelation, we will no longer see through a glass darkly, but have perfect vision and knowledge on God's purposes with no more conflict, division, or tears. We *can* have certainty now that God loves *all* people and desires them to be saved. For God shows no partiality. [2]

We walk in freedom if we are being transformed by his truth. Freedom comes in letting go of interior bondage through forgiveness, letting go of resentment, and confession. The Lord gave us the Beatitudes to purify our self-centeredness and lead us to mercy and compassion. He did not give us the Be-aptitudes, so we will not grow in virtue relying on our natural talents. Our hearts are free when we let go of the appearance of holiness when we are *not* and confess when God shows us our innermost parts. He is healing our denial and love of self. Isaiah reacts in confession when the Holy One comes near with Truth.

Woe is me! For I am lost; for I am a man of unclean lips, and I dwell in a midst of a people of unclean lips; for my eyes have seen the King, the LORD of hosts! [3]

If we hold on to our defenses and hide in the garden, our hearts are sad, angry, and avoidant. If we confess, our joy is restored and renewed energy to reach out to others. We connect easier as self-consciousness fades. Our dance company performed a ballet on being back in the garden. God breathed into our lifeless bodies, and we were redeemed and renewed after the fall through Christ. Edith Stein said, "In order to be an image of God, the spirit must turn to what is eternal, hold it in spirit, keep it in memory, and by loving it, embrace it in the will." It is painful to leave the pain of hovering over our need to control our lives but worth letting go of the illusion of power. Underneath control is always fear. Freedom is in letting go of hiding from the love of God and others!

1	John 8:32
2	Romans 2:11
3	Isaiah 6:5

My reflections.
Lectio, reading the Scripture...slowly

Meditation, drawn to these words...

Prayer of the heart...

Contemplation...silence

Friends

No longer do I call you servants, for the servant does not know what his master is doing; but I have called you friends, for all that I have heard from my Father I have made known to you. [1]

Being a friend of Jesus means he shares his plans with us, and it is our free choice to enter or remain distant as a servant only. He shares what he is doing in gentle ways to allow us to do good works for God's glory.

Are we being a friend who shares our plans and thoughts? Do we encourage, forgive, listen, and reciprocate? Or compete, boast, hold on to resentment, and not listen? We fail the test in being the best friend Jesus is to us, but we can grow in becoming a supportive, and faithful one.

Two are better than one, because they have a good reward for their toil. Or if they fall, one will lift up his fellow; but woe to him who is alone when he falls and has not another to lift him up. [2]

A good friend sacrifices time and energy, but we cannot comprehend the greatest love. Greater love has no man than this, that a man lay down his life for his friends. [3] Jesus also did not trust himself to everyone. We can be cautious but careful not to judge or ostracize others unlike ourselves.

But Jesus did not trust himself to them, because he knew all men and needed no one to bear witness to man; for he himself knew what was in man. [4]

We unconsciously look for friends like ourselves but are also blessed with ones who are different and complement us. We are a friend within a marriage, as a parent, sister, and daughter. Lord, help us see our blind ways to avoid hurting our friends. If the one you trust is competitive, contentious, or does not encourage, this is not a friend. Jesus is perfect love, and perfect love casts out fear. So, if we trust him, we are free to enter new friendships and restore old ones if possible. *When* we are hurt again, we can forgive.

We can become extravagant lovers as joyful women because our deepest need for love is met! Whom have I in heaven but thee? And there is nothing on earth that I desire besides thee. [5]

1   John 15:15
2   Ecclesiastes 4:9,10
3   John 15:13
4   John 2:24, 25
5   Psalm 73:25

My reflections.
Lectio, reading the Scripture...slowly

Meditation, drawn to these words...

Prayer of the heart...

Contemplation...silence

Family

A father of the fatherless and defender of the widows, is God in his holy habitation.
God sets the lonely in families. He brings out the prisoners with singing,
but the rebellious dwell in a sun-scorched land. [1]

A joyful family is coming! Whether our earthly family is loving, supportive, detached, or combative, until we see him face to face, we will feel the lack of perfect parental love. God promised that despite our circumstance or history, he is *unfailing* love.

The lines have fallen for me in pleasant places; yea, I have a goodly heritage. [2]

Our needs and desires will be met by our Lover.
"And in that day, says the LORD, you will call me, 'My husband,'
and no longer will you call me 'My Baal.' [3]

Our souls will know full happiness. As we wait for the perfect to come, he is as close as our breath. We can cry "hold me, Jesus."

Our Blessed Mother is our strongest intercessor.
"Then he said to the disciple, "Behold, your mother!" [4]

We will be with the holy family and all the angels and saints.
And he replied, "Who are my mother and my brethren?" And looking around
on those who sat about him, he said, "Here are my mother and my brethren!
Whoever does the will of God is my brother, and sister, and mother." [5]

Therefore, since we are surrounded by so great a cloud of witnesses, let
us also lay aside every weight and the sin that clings so closely, and
let us run with perseverance the race that is set before us. [6]

We will be singing together with the heavenly host community!
The twenty-four elders fall before the one who is seated on the
throne and worship the one who lives forever and ever; they cast

their crowns before the throne, singing, "You are worthy, our Lord
and God, to receive glory and honor and power, for you created
all things, and by our will they existed and were created." [7]

1   Psalm 68:5,6
2   Psalm 16:6
3   Hosea 2:16
4   John 19:27
5   Mark 3:33-35
6   Romans 12:1, 2
7   Revelation 4:10, 11

My reflections.
Lectio, reading the Scripture...slowly

Meditation, drawn to these words...

Prayer of the heart...

Contemplation...silence

Children

But Jesus called them to him, saying, "Let the children come to me, and do not hinder them;
for to such belongs the kingdom of God. Truly, I say to you, whoever does not receive
the kingdom of God like a child shall not enter it." [1]

We hear *joy* in the heart of God for the children! Jesus' delight for their trusting souls reveals his love for purity. If we see God face to face, it will be as a child in dependence, innocence, humility, and transparency. Many of our attitudes developed through education, work, and personal goals will be purified to see him. He clearly confronts our need to repent and become like children. We can safely let go of hiding to relate more genuinely like a child because *he* is our safety.

Having the mind of Christ also means having a welcoming heart for the children, and he plainly confronts our presumption that we are more important. We are the proud ones with our talents, credentials, and accomplishments. We can watch their souls to see what God loves and confess our pride to regain our innocence.

Children are a gift from the Lord. The human person is God's creation and gift above all things, and we are all created for his good pleasure. If we have no time for the children and dismiss them as annoyances, we are blind and misguided. We are not to hinder the children from coming to him, but to bless and help them through life. Any other attitude towards children meets Jesus' stern rebuke. Parents' sins against their children beg for divine mercy as he speaks strong words for their protection.

Women who are not called to a vocation of mother but have other assignments and spiritual children serve with enthusiasm and great joy. When there *are* many little olive shoots around the table, it may be messy and loud, but mothers feel joy in the chaos. They rattle off little olive shoot names without pausing. Glory to God!

Your wife will be like a fruitful vine within your house;
your children will be like olive shoots around your table. [2]

1   Luke 18:16, 17
2   Psalm 128:3

My reflections.
Lectio, reading the Scripture...slowly

Meditation, drawn to these words...

Prayer of the heart...

Contemplation...silence

Beauty

Behold, you are beautiful, my love, behold, you are beautiful! Your eyes are doves behind your veil.
Your hair is like a flock of goats, moving down the slopes of Gilead. Your lips are like a scarlet thread,
and your mouth is lovely. Your cheeks are like halves of a pomegranate behind your veil. [1]

Our desire to be beautiful is from God. He repeats his delight in our beauty so that we know. He knows every detail of our body and soul as bridegroom. We are quick to criticize ourselves over physical flaws and inner weaknesses, but we can safely see ourselves as he sees us and not with our shaming voice or others'.

You are all fair, my love; there is no flaw in you. [2]

We are all created in beauty and reflect God's own beauty. St. Thomas Aquinas said, "The divine beauty is that from which all being is derived." Your voice, features, and soul attract him.

Worthy art thou, our Lord and God, to receive glory and honor and power,
for thou didst create all things, and by thy will they existed and were created. [3]

St. Augustine pursued the Lord himself after years of pursuing only the physically attractive. He reflected in <u>Confessions,</u> "Belatedly I loved Thee, O Beauty, so ancient and so new, belatedly I loved Thee. For see, Thou wast within and I was without, and I sought thee out there. Unlovely, I rushed heedlessly among the lovely things Thou hast made. Thou wast with me, but I was not with Thee. These things kept me far from Thee; even though they were not at all unless they were in Thee."

Our self-image could become *his* image of us, which is accurate, not more or less. We can be emotionally free from bowing our heads in self-hatred or using our bodies for seduction and self-glorification. I have seen wounded women after surgically modifying their bodies only to be abandoned by the one they lured from another woman. They were used as simply the next beauty instead of a beloved bride. No more self-consciousness, self-loathing,

envy, or competition is necessary to feel accepted and loved. I am my beloved's and my beloved is mine; [4]

1   Song of Solomon 4:1,3
2   Song of Solomon 4:7
3   Revelation 4:11
4   Song of Solomon 6:3a

My reflections.
Lectio, reading the Scripture...slowly

Meditation, drawn to these words...

Prayer of the heart...

Contemplation...silence

Joy of the Beloved

Intimacy

He who has my commandments and keeps them, he it is who loves me;
and he who loves me will be loved by my Father,
a and I will love him and manifest myself to him. [1]

What happens interiorly when we intentionally *stay* in his love and obey what he has spoken? Jesus manifests himself to us. We gaze, and his love comes closer only by his grace and in many ways. St. Teresa of Avila, Carmelite, and Doctor of the Church, experienced this manifestation after reading Augustine's <u>Confessions.</u> She longed for more intimacy and waited.

She wrote about a vision of an angel piercing her heart,
"The pain was so great, that it made me moan; and yet so surpassing was the sweetness of this excessive pain, that I could not wish to be rid of it. The soul is satisfied with nothing less than God. The pain is not bodily, but spiritual. It is a caressing of love so sweet which now takes place between the soul and God, that I pray God of His goodness to make him experience it who may think that I am lying." [2]

Not being aware of some things our Lord has spoken can create distance in our relationship with him. We can feel detached or become scrupulous from failing to understand and accept his grace.
For as the heavens are higher than the earth, so are my ways higher than your ways and my thoughts than your thoughts. [3]

Pope St. Gregory the Great wrote in 590AD, "Study, I beg you, and each day meditate on the words of your Creator. Learn the heart of God in the words of God, so that you long more ardently for eternity." [4]. Our obedience leads to this manifestation of his love. Through his still, small voice, he speaks to us through Scripture, Mass, quiet contemplation, dreams, angels, music, nature, and people. He sees the desire of our heart to obey, intentions, sacrifices to obey, diligence in duties, devotions, silence, spiritual readings, and prayer for others.

1   John 14:21
2   Aleteia.org
3   Isaiah 55:9
4   www.catholicapologetics.org The Teachings of the Catholic Church: On Reading the Bible

My reflections.
Lectio, reading the Scripture...slowly

Meditation, drawn to these words...

Prayer of the heart...

Contemplation...silence

Mercy

And his mercy is on those who fear him from generation to generation. [1]

More good news. Did you know we are also not cast out of his protection when we do *not* do what he says? When we have not stayed in his love or prayed enough or have not been loving to our neighbor, God's ear is still attentive and answers our cries. He protects us when we forget to ask because he knows our needs better than we do.

Before they call I will answer, while they are yet speaking I will hear. [2]

His angels are dispatched for our protection, and the communion of the saints pray on our behalf. Our Blessed Mother never fails to intercede for us, and his divine mercy is always reaching for us. He understands and knows how to reach us in our blindness.

Do you not know that God's kindness is meant to lead you to repentance? [3]

Jesus despised the shame of his passion. The agony, scourging, crowning of thorns, and carrying his cross were not worthy of the glory to be revealed. There is no need to live in shame or hide in the garden because he sees it all. He calls us into the light while we are still in darkness.

For we have not a high priest who is unable to sympathize with our weaknesses, but one who in every respect has been tempted as we are, yet without sin. [4]

He does not treat us as our sins deserve! Glory to God.

He *is* Divine Mercy. He does not deal with us according to our sins, nor requite us according to our iniquities. For as the heavens are high above the earth, so great is his steadfast love toward those who fear him; as far as the east is from the west, so far does he remove our transgressions from us. As a father pities his children, so the LORD pities those who fear him. For he knows our frame; he remembers that we are dust. [5]

Only his strong love shatters our shame and sets us free! Principles, therapists, and knowledge do not heal, but help unravel problems. God is our Healer, and Mary is the Undoer of Knots!

1   Luke 1:50
2   Psalm 65:24
3   Romans 2:4
4   Hebrews 4:15
5   Psalm 103:10-14

My reflections.
Lectio, reading the Scripture...slowly

Meditation, drawn to these words...

Prayer of the heart...

Contemplation...silence

Forgiveness

For if you forgive men their trespasses, your heavenly Father also will forgive you;
but if you do not forgive men their trespasses, neither will your
Father forgive your trespasses. [1]

Joy erupts in us when we confess and forgive. Everything. We are all the wounder and the wounded, so grievances happen on all sides. If we are aware someone has something against us, we are to initiate being forgiven and restore relationship if possible. Being received depends on the humility of the offended and is not our responsibility.

> leave your gift there before the altar and go; first be reconciled
> to your brother, and then come and offer your gift. [2]

Forgiving the offender heals us from resentment and need for revenge regardless of the offense. Circumstances may not change but emotions focused backward start to fade, and we are no longer in bondage. Forgiveness may take years, but we confess unlimited times in the present or in our memory.

> Lord, how often shall my brother sin against me, and I forgive
> him? As many as seven times? Jesus said to him, "I do not
> say to you seven times, but seventy times seven." [3]

We are not called to be in close relationship with everyone, but always to forgive and restore if possible. Pope John XXIII said, "See everything, overlook a great deal, correct a little."

> If possible, so far as it depends on you, be at peace with all people. [4]

When someone does not cease to create division or danger, God can show us when to be silent, speak, trust, or engage.

> Or not. Too long have I had my dwelling among those who hate peace.
> I am for peace; but when I speak, they are for war. [5]

Jesus remained silent in accusations, yet he raged at pharisees, overturned tables, and warned those who abused children. We can completely forgive someone and yet not trust them if behavior does not change. No offense, however, is too great to forgive as he has forgiven us. He is Divine Mercy!

1   Matthew 6:14-15
2   Matthew 5:24
3   Matthew 18:21-22
4   Romans 12:18
5   Psalm 120:6

My reflections.
Lectio, reading the Scripture...slowly

Meditation, drawn to these words...

Prayer of the heart...

Contemplation...silence

Thanksgiving

And he took bread, and when he had given thanks he broke it and gave it to them, saying,
"This is my body which is given for you. Do this in remembrance of me."
And likewise the cup after supper, saying, "This cup which is poured
out for you is the new covenant in my blood. [1]

St. John Vianney said, "If we really understood the Mass, we would die of joy." The Eucharist is a sacrifice of thanksgiving to the Father, a blessing by which the Church expresses her gratitude to God for all his benefits, for all that he has accomplished through creation, redemption, and sanctification. Eucharist means first of all "thanksgiving." [2] The mystery of faith produces joy as we offer back to God the Body and Blood of our Lord Jesus.

He knew this hard saying was being murmured about, and his vulnerable question about their choice to leave broke my heart. Jesus *would* be this vulnerable and non-demanding out of respect for our free will. He asked about their commitment and let them go with no pleading or consequence. He felt abandoned but did not confront. His love accepts our choices even knowing consequences await us. He lets us process and decide, but his love is always pursuing. His reaction brought me to confession about reacting in misunderstandings and abandonment.

His *literal* language is often rejected here though accepted about the virgin birth and Jesus' miracles. I understood St. Peter when my own eyes were opened to this strange idea without full comprehension. Peter heard the truth and trusted the Lord's eternal words despite his mental objections. My mind and spirit were reconciled through the mystery of faith. I understood why our Thanksgiving, the Eucharist, is "the source and summit of the Christian life." [3] This was no longer a doctrine to be debated but became my daily bread.

After this many of his disciples drew back and no longer went about with him. Jesus said to the twelve, "Will you also go away?" Simon Peter answered him, "Lord, to whom shall we go? You have the words of eternal life;" [4]

1	Luke 22:19, 20
2	CCC 1360
3	CCC 1324
4	John 6:66-68

My reflections.
Lectio, reading the Scripture...slowly

Meditation, drawn to these words...

Prayer of the heart...

Contemplation...silence

Confession

Jesus said to them again, "Peace be with you. As the Father has sent me, even so I send you."
And when he had said this, he breathed on them, and said to them, "Receive the Holy Spirit.
If you forgive the sins of any, they are forgiven; if you retain the sins of any, they are retained." [1]

Praise God for his reconciling us to himself. The Sacrament of Confession brings joy and healing as he restores our relationship with him through forgiveness. As he breathed on the apostles his authority to forgive sins, we are freed from the guilt and shame of our sins as we confess. The peace we receive is a great grace helping us persevere and abide in his love. We confess to God directly as well as the Holy Spirit prompts us.

> If we confess our sins, he is faithful and just and will forgive
> us our sins and purify us from all unrighteousness. [2]

In our desire to restore relationship, humility is needed to hear others' grievances against us. Defensiveness is a sign of pride as we minimize our wounds against others. If the harm is done to us, we can approach the offender, but if our efforts fail, we can let it hurt and let it go. We cannot be emotionally demanding without offending God and can forgive them without their confession. Forgiveness sets them free and is healing for us. If we seek restoration through the Church and efforts fail, we are encouraged to disassociate from the repeated offender.

> If your brother sins against you, go and tell him his fault, between you
> and him alone. If he listens to you, you have gained your brother. But
> if he does not listen, take one or two others along with you, that every
> word may be confirmed by the evidence of two or three witnesses. If he
> refuses to listen to them, tell it to the church; and if he refuses to listen
> even to the church, let him to be you as a Gentile and a tax collector. [3]

When acceptance is offered to those who are despised and rejected by others, the kindness of God can lead them to repentance.

Or do you presume upon the riches of his kindness and forbearance and patience: Do you not know that God's kindness is meant to lead you to repentance? [4]

1   John 20:21-24
2   I John 1:9
3   Matthew 18:15-17
4   Romans 2:4

My reflections.
Lectio, reading the Scripture...slowly

Meditation, drawn to these words...

Prayer of the heart...

Contemplation...silence

Healing

He has sent me to proclaim release to the captives and recovering of sight to the blind, to set at liberty those who are oppressed, [1]

There is great joy in healing!
But for you who fear my name the sun of righteousness arises with healing
    in his wings. You shall go forth leaping like calves from the stall. [2]
Jesus heals us spiritually, gradually, and instantaneously!
    And leaping up he stood and walked and entered the temple
    with them, walking and leaping and praising God. [3]
Jesus healed because of his compassion and for the glory of God!
how God anointed Jesus of Nazareth with the Holy Spirit and with power;
how he went about doing good and healing all that were oppressed by the devil,
    for God was with him. [4]

St. Teresa of Avila wrote, "We always find that those who walked closest to Christ were those who had to bear the greatest trials." In physical and emotional suffering, Jesus is close to the brokenhearted. Darkness despises his beloveds who live in his presence, but the accuser will be thrown down.
    Now the salvation and the power and the kingdom of our God and the
    authority of his Christ have come, for the accuser of our brethren has
    been thrown down, who accuses them day and night before our God. [5]

Though the saints were grieved for false accusations, his will was accomplished through them, and they forgave their accusers.
    St. Bernadette of Lourdes was ridiculed and accused of lying by authorities
    and her family for fabricating recurring visions of the Blessed Mother and
    instructions to dig in the dirt at a grotto in France in 1858. As a result of
    her humility and obedience, a healing spring resulted in seventy people

having instantaneous healings (1862-2018). [6] These have been scientifically validated, investigated, and approved by the Church under strict guidelines. Another 7,000 have had unexplained cures after leaving Lourdes. [7]

1   Luke 4:18b
2   Malachi 4:2
3   Acts 3:8
4   Acts 10:38
5   Revelation 12:10
6   Fr. Robert Spitzer, S.J., PhD, blog.magiscenter.com.
7   Contemporary Scientifically Validated Miracles Associated with Blessed Mary, Saints and the Holy Eucharist. Pages 6-13. https://f.hubspotusercontent40.net lourdes-france.org

My reflections.
Lectio, reading the Scripture...slowly

Meditation, drawn to these words...

Prayer of the heart...

Contemplation...silence

Compassion

*And Jesus went about all the cities and villages, teaching in their synagogues
and preaching the gospel of the kingdom, and healing every disease and every infirmity.
When he saw the crowds, he had compassion for them, because they were harassed
and helpless, like sheep without a shepherd.* [1]

Jesus' compassion moves him to tears for our suffering individually and corporately. Many world problems seem to be beyond our control, but he knows our helplessness and is with us in our fears and insecurities.

Thou hast kept count of my tossings; put thou my tears in thy bottle!
Are they not in thy book? [2]

St. Teresa of Avila wrote, "Christ has nobody now on earth but yours, no hands but yours, no feet but yours. Yours are the eyes through which to look out Christ's compassion to the world. Yours are the feet with which he is to go about doing good; Yours are the hands with which he is to bless men now."

And behold, two blind men sitting by the road, when they heard that Jesus
was passing by, cried out, "Have mercy on us, Son of David!" And Jesus
stopped and called them, saying, "What do you want me to do for you?"
They said to him, "Lord, let our eyes be opened." And Jesus in pity touched
their eyes, and immediately they received their sight and followed him. [3]

If we are women infused with the holy joy of Jesus, we also are filled with his compassion for people. When we are free to love as he loves, we can express love for each other in loss. Help us be willing, O Lord, to not avoid those suffering around us for fear of not knowing what to say or how to help. Just sitting in the darkness with someone is compassionate and life-giving.

We do not have the power, but Jesus does, and we may intercede for our friends, family, or strangers to see healing because of his great compassion! Ask in faith. Be persistent. Be expectant. He is listening.
He is waiting.

1   Matthew 9:35, 36
2   Psalm 56:8
3   Matthew 20:30-34

My reflections.
Lectio, reading the Scripture...slowly

Meditation, drawn to these words...

Prayer of the heart...

Contemplation...silence

Silence

"Be still, and know that I am God. I am exalted among the nations, I am exalted in the earth!"
The Lord of hosts is with us; the God of Jacob is our refuge. [1]

Silence is our response in the presence of God's majesty.
When the Lamb opened the seventh seal, there was silence in heaven
for about half an hour. [2]

But the LORD is in his holy temple; let all the earth keep silence before him. [3]

And all the assembly kept silence; and they listened to
Barnabas and Paul as they related what signs and wonders
God had done through them among the Gentiles. [4]

Silence is our response when he commands us to be silent.
The LORD will fight for you, and you have only to be still. [5]

Be angry, but sin not; commune with your own
hearts on your beds, and be silent. [6]

Give heed, O Job, listen to me; be silent, and I will speak. [7]

And he awoke and rebuked the wind, and said to the sea, "Peace! Be still!"
And the wind ceased, and there was a great calm. [8]

Silence is the Lord's response in false accusations.
Now the passage of the scripture which he was reading was this:
"As a sheep led to the slaughter or a lamb before its shearer is dumb,
so he opens not his mouth. [9]

But he gave him no answer, not even to a single charge;
so that the governor wondered greatly. [10]

Sometimes we speak; sometimes we are to be silent.
> A time to tear apart and a time to sew together;
> A time to be silent and a time to speak. [11]

> And he earnestly warned them not to tell who he was. [12]

1   Psalm 46:10, 11
2   Revelation 8:1
3   Habakkuk 2:20
4   Acts 15:12
5   Exodus 14:14
6   Psalm 4:4
7   Job 33:31
8   Mark 4:39
9   Acts 8:32
10   Matthew 27:14
11   Ecclesiastes 3:7
12   Mark 3:12

My reflections.
Lectio, reading the Scripture...slowly

Meditation, drawn to these words...

Prayer of the heart...

Contemplation...silence

Prayer

Pray at all times in the Spirit, with all prayer and supplication. [1]

Jesus said our reward in prayer happens in secrecy.
> But when you pray, go into your room and shut the door and pray to
> your Father who is in secret; and your Father who sees in secret will
> reward you. And in praying do not heap up empty phrases as the Gentiles
> do; for they think that they will be heard for their many words. [2]

After the Lord's prayer, Jesus taught the disciples the importance of persistence. And I tell you, Ask, and it will be given you; seek, and you will find; knock, and it will be opened to you. For everyone who asks receives, and he who seeks finds, and to him who knocks it will be opened. What father among you, if his son asks for a fish, will instead of a fish give him a serpent; or if he asks for an egg, will give him a scorpion? [3]

Staying in his love answers prayers.
> If you abide in me, and my words abide in you, ask
> whatever you will, and it shall be done for you. [4]

God wants our heart and responds to honesty, tears, and intercession. King David cried, I am weary with my moaning; every night I flood my bed with tears; I drench my couch with my weeping. [5]

The Rosary is our powerful prayer and weapon. Martin Luther knew Mary as our spiritual mother and intercessor. He wrote, "She is full of grace, proclaimed to be entirely without sin—something exceedingly great. For God's grace fills her with everything good and makes her devoid of all evil. It is the consolation and the superabundant goodness of God, that man is able to exult in such a treasure. Mary is the Mother of Jesus and the Mother of all of us even though it was Christ alone who reposed on her knees." [6]

He cleanses us from the day in the prayer of examen by St. Ignatius of Loyola. We review the day, trust God's grace and forgiveness, and decide to be more conscious of our words and actions.

> O Lord, thou hast searched me and known me! Thou knowest when I sit down and rise up; thou discernest my thoughts from afar. Thou searchest out my path and my lying down, and art acquainted with all my ways. [7]

1   Ephesians 6:18a
2   Matthew 6:6, 7
3   Luke 11:9-12
4   John 15:7
5   Psalm 6:6
6   https://catholicbridge.com
7   Psalm 139:1-3

My reflections.
Lectio, reading the Scripture...slowly

Meditation, drawn to these words...

Prayer of the heart...

Contemplation...silence

Peace

Peace I leave with you; my peace I give to you; not as the world gives do I give to you.
Let not your hearts be troubled, neither let them be afraid. [1]

We want true peace from Jesus who will sustain us until we see him face to face.

> And let the peace of Christ rule in your hearts, to which indeed
> you were called in the one body. And be thankful. [2]

If peace is the rule in our heart, we can be intentional to seek it with others and avoid mingling with those who thrive on division. St. Teresa of Avila said, "Let nothing disturb you, Let nothing frighten you, Though all things pass, God does not change. Patience wins all things. But he lacks nothing who possesses God; For God alone suffices."

St. Augustine wrote, "I was drawn to the peace I found in virtue, and repelled by the rancor I found in vice, attributing the former to unity, the latter to division." Peace follows truth, and false peace is a temporary illusion. We do not want the world's peace to feel calm through denial, consumerism, self-soothing, entertainment, addictions, sex, or proclamations of peace when there is no peace.

> Steadfast love and faithfulness will meet; righteousness
> and peace will kiss each other. [3]

We lose our peace when we stray from God's Word.

> Why then has this people turned away in perpetual backsliding? They hold fast
> to deceit; they refuse to return. I have given heed and listened, but they have not
> spoken aright; no man repents of his wickedness, saying, "What have I done?"
> Everyone turns to his own course, like a horse plunging headlong into battle. [4]

Yet, why did Jesus tell us he did not come to bring peace but a sword? Do not think that I have come to bring peace on earth;
I have not come to bring peace, but a sword. [5]

He was warning about division in families and attacks we would face if we lived according to his truth. We can trust knowing the King of Kings and Lord of Lords left us with *his* peace!

1   John 14:27
2   Colossians 3:15
3   Psalm 85:10
4   Jeremiah 8:5, 6
5   Matthew 10:34

My reflections.
Lectio, reading the Scripture...slowly

Meditation, drawn to these words...

Prayer of the heart...

Contemplation...silence

Joy of the Virtues

Humility

But he gives more grace; therefore it says, "God opposes the proud, but gives grace to the humble." [1]

God resists us if we are living in pride and self-glorification.

Purify our hearts, Lord, to live and work for your glory. Humility happens as we love God. We worship and focus on him instead of obsessing on our virtue of humility. St. Alphonsus Liguori said, "A soul that is truly humble refuses her own praise, and should praises be bestowed upon her, she refers them all to God." Mary's Magnificat reveals her joy that God chose her to be the Mother of God and accepted her assignment as a humble woman called to do his will.

Mary's heart was childlike and did not consider her reputation, suffering, or the unknowns. She never looked back. Humility was the main virtue causing her to say Yes to God's will for her life. She was *full* of grace and holy joy when she visited Elizabeth, and her joy was in giving her life away to divine providence. Our Blessed Mother recognized the great honor in being chosen to bear the Messiah, but her humility pointed to Jesus, her Savior.

> And Mary said, "My soul magnifies the Lord, and my spirit rejoices in
> God my Savior, for he has regarded the low estate of his handmaiden.
> For behold, henceforth all generations will call me blessed; [2]

Mary received hard words from Simeon's blessing that she would suffer great emotional distress from words spoken against her child. Yet, she was faithful and trusted God for her future.

> Then Simeon blessed them and said to Mary, his mother: "This child
> is destined to cause the falling and rising of many in Israel, and to be
> a sign that will be spoken against, so that the thoughts of many hearts
> will be revealed. And a sword will pierce your own soul too." [3]

St. Teresa of Avila said, "We shall never learn to know ourselves except by endeavoring to know God; for, beholding his greatness, we realize our own littleness; his purity shows us our foulness; and by meditating upon his humility, we find how very far we are from being humble."

1   James 4:6
2   Luke 1:46,47,48
3   Luke 2:34, 35

My reflections.
Lectio, reading the Scripture...slowly

Meditation, drawn to these words...

Prayer of the heart...

Contemplation...silence

Purity

Blessed are the pure in heart, for they shall see God. [1]

"Pure in heart" refers to those who have attuned their intellects and wills to the demands of God's holiness, chiefly in three areas: charity; chastity or sexual rectitude; love of truth and orthodoxy of faith. There is a connection between purity of heart, of body, and of faith" [2] Pope Benedict stated, "To be capable of seeing God, the powers of our soul must be purified and reintegrated." As we become more abandoned, we can let go of fear and resentment and become like a trusting child.

Our heart is purified when we die to the hidden activities of competition, envy, gossip, and criticizing the trivial actions of others in the lower soul as St. Teresa of Avila taught in <u>The Interior Castle</u>. Our own holiness is the focus. [3] Because we are all the wounded and the wounder, we can extend the same mercy we are given. Instead of judging our neighbors and insisting on our ways of engaging in the world, we can spend energy sowing love for God's glory through acceptance and understanding.

Edith Stein left academia and became Sr. Teresa Benedicta of the Cross after reading St. Teresa of Avila's writings. She experienced conversion of the heart and refocused her philosophical studies on theology after a life in academia before her martyrdom at Auschwitz. Her earlier teachings on empathy showed her desire to understand how to know another person and led to a deeper thirst for God.

Edith wrote to women on detachment and mortal concerns within the soul being consumed by the fire of God's love in contemplation. [4] She said, "Let go of your plans. The first hour of your morning belongs to God. Tackle the day's work that he charges you with, and he will give you the power to accomplish it." [5] Purity happens when we adore and live for him.

1   Matthew 5:8
2   CCC 2518
3   www.sacred-texts.com Interior Castle, 19-22
4   Edith Stein Essays on Woman
5   www.inspiringquotes.us

My reflections.
Lectio, reading the Scripture...slowly

Meditation, drawn to these words...

Prayer of the heart...

Contemplation...silence

Faith

We walk by faith, and not by sight. [1]

The virtue of faith means "one who trusts." The three theological virtues of faith, hope, and love work together to bring glory to God in daily sacrificial love. Blaise Pascal, French physicist, inventor, writer, and Catholic theologian said, "The heart has its reasons which reason knows nothing of. We know the truth not only by the reason, but by the heart." Faith and reason are not in contradiction according to St. Thomas Aquinas who stated, "Jesus said we can believe him based upon his authority *or* on his works. In other words, miracles provide evidence for our rational faculties that what is being said by a divine truth-giver is in fact true."[2]

Grace and faith are *both* necessary for our salvation. Grace is freely given, and by faith we cooperate with his grace. Without his grace, we would be lost with no path to reconciliation.

For by grace you have been saved through faith; and this is not your own doing; it is the gift of God--not because of works, lest any man should boast. [3]

St. Paul also teaches good works from the (*mosaic*) law do *not* merit salvation, as in circumcision. We do *not* work ourselves to heaven through good deeds outlined in the Old Testament Law.

For we hold that a man is justified by faith apart from works of the law. [4]

However, the works of *love* Jesus taught in the sheep and goats parable *are* necessary for salvation and flow out of our *faith working through love.* For in Christ Jesus neither circumcision nor uncircumcision is of any avail, but faith working through love. [5] These works of charity accompany faith and grace. Jesus, James, and Paul all teach clearly that faith and works of love allow us to enter eternal life. Faith alone is not sufficient. You see that a man is justified by works and not by faith alone. [6] God knows those who have faith, works of charity, are in friendship with him, and free from mortal sin at the hour of our death. We do not. Forgive our presumption, O Lord.

Glory to God, Our Divine Mercy!

1   II Cor. 5:7
2   St. Thomas Aquinas Summa Contra Gentiles, Book 1, chapter 7. www.genius.com
3   Ephesians 2:8-9
4   Roman 3:28
5   Galatians 5:6
6   James 2:24

My reflections.
Lectio, reading the Scripture...slowly

Meditation, drawn to these words...

Prayer of the heart...

Contemplation...silence

Hope

For in this hope we were saved. Now hope that is seen is not hope.
For who hopes for what he sees?
But if we hope for what we do not see, we wait for it with patience. [1]

Hope is a gift given to us. Along with faith and love, hope is a theological virtue which St. Thomas Aquinas said is "infused into our souls by God alone, as also, finally, because we come to know of them only by Divine revelation in the Sacred Scriptures." [2] Hope keeps us looking toward the joy set before us just as Jesus' hope was set on the joy ahead sitting at his Father's right hand.

I see excellent women lose hope in staying above the line of despair when problems remain unresolved. A joyful spirit may sit in aimless depression, stripped of her self-reliance and ability to heal herself, and wait for him to help. Only hindsight can reveal how powerful God was in the dark night of the soul. This may feel like despair, but it is not. It is deep discouragement.

The Catechism clarifies hope from despair which has an attitude of defiance. Hope is the confident expectation of divine blessing and the beatific vision of God. [3] "By despair, man ceases to hope for his personal salvation from God, for help in attaining it or for the forgiveness of his sins. Despair is contrary to God's goodness, to his justice—for the Lord is faithful to his promises—and to his mercy." [4] Despair has elements of presumption hoping to save himself or presuming upon God's mercy without conversion. [5]

Pope Benedict's encyclical letter on hope, Spe Salvi, states the connection between hope and faith. He says the "Gospel is not merely a communication of things that can be known—it is one that makes things happen and is life-changing. The dark door of time, of the future has been thrown open.

The one who hopes has been granted the gift of a new life." [6] Glory to God in the highest!

1   Romans 8:24, 25
2   Summa Theologica (ST I-II.62.1)
3   Catechism of the Catholic Church Part 3 Section 2, 2090
4   Catechism of the Catholic Church Part 3 Section 2, 2091
5   Catechism of the Catholic Church Part 3 Section 2, 2092
6   Encyclical Letter Spe Salvi of the Supreme Pontiff Benedict XVI; 2. Faith is Hope.

My reflections.
Lectio, reading the Scripture...slowly

Meditation, drawn to these words...

Prayer of the heart...

Contemplation...silence

Boldness

*And now, Lord, look upon their threats, and grant to thy servants
to speak thy word with all boldness,* [1]

Do you feel fire inside to speak but say nothing from fear of rejection, being misunderstood, or unsure if the Holy Spirit is the source? I do constantly. If the message is prompted by the Holy Spirit, the virtue of boldness helps us bypass the fear to speak. We are all learning when to speak or be silent out of love and respect. The virtue of boldness grows and helps us overcome fear to defend, protect, and proclaim God's Truth and concerns.

Certainty on issues according to our own lens and authority is self-righteousness. Uncertainty in conversation allows all to be heard and understood as God's children. If God has spoken, his Truth is non-negotiable, and we may be called to be bold and speak with certainty in awkward moments to protect vulnerable souls. The challenge is hearing his voice accurately! We all tend to be right in our own eyes.

Confronting evil can risk the loss of relationships, and more persecution may be the consequence for speaking his Truth. We pray to hear his voice, discernment of spirits, and protection from self-righteousness and deception.

St. Catherine of Siena devoted her life to unity as a contemplative activist, mystic, and writer in the 1300's and showed great boldness in pursuing leaders to establish peace. She worked to promote peace in the political world after a life of serving her family as the 25th child of her mother in 1347. St. Catherine urged peace in Italy and the Church during the war by appealing to Pope Gregory XI to return to Rome while exiled in Avignon. Her strength and boldness caused him to entrust her with the task of negotiating peace.

Catherine later wrote on prayer in The Dialogue of St. Catherine of Siena, Divine Providence. She was declared patron saint of Rome in 1866 and a doctor of the Church in 1970 by Pope Paul VI. [2]

1   Acts 4:29
2   En.m.wikipedia.org/wiki/CatherineofSiena

My reflections.
Lectio, reading the Scripture...slowly

Meditation, drawn to these words...

Prayer of the heart...

Contemplation...silence

Endurance

You will be hated by all for my name's sake. But not a hair of your head will perish. By your endurance you will gain your lives. [1]

Strength comes from joy in the heart of God and gives determination to endure hard things. Women like Ruth have endured responsibilities to the point of exhaustion, whatever it takes. Sacrificial love motivated her to work hard physically and care for Naomi without worrying about the costs. She was abandoned to God for her assignment to endure the will of God.

> Then Boaz said to his servant who was in charge of the reapers, "Whose maiden is this?" She said, 'Pray, let me glean and gather among the sheaves after the reapers.' So she came, and she has continued from early morning until now, without resting even for a moment." [2]

Endurance happens with training of the soul and body, and women like the challenge to see fruit of their labor in serving, caretaking, creating, working, and exercising. We run the race of life to get an eternal crown, not a temporary one, and our ability to complete the task involves grace and our will.

> Do you not know that in a race all the runners run, but only one gets the prize? Run in such a way as to get the prize. Everyone who competes in the games goes into strict training. They do it to get a crown that will not last, but we do it to get a crown that will last forever. [3]

We need self-discipline and want to discern the assignment until he changes our direction. Most assignments are obvious as life unfolds and being flexible is important when he adjusts our focus. He can remove distractions we may see as necessities for life to get our attention. Pain and suffering are usually the path to the goal.

Seasons change, and we go where he leads. We can hold earthly things loosely and grow in endurance from the changes he allows. At the end of our lives, we will have peace as he reminds us of the small races we ran faithfully and assurance he is with us after the long one is won. Let's persevere to the end. *He* is our reward.

1   Luke 21:19
2   Ruth 2:5,7
3   I Cor. 9:24-27

My reflections.
Lectio, reading the Scripture...slowly

Meditation, drawn to these words...

Prayer of the heart...

Contemplation...silence

Prudence

For she is an initiate in the knowledge of God, and an associate in his works.
If riches are a desirable possession in life, what is richer than
wisdom who effects all things? [1]

St. Thomas Aquinas said prudence is wisdom concerning human affairs[2] or right reason with respect to action. [3] Prudence helps us decide on a course of action through counsel, judgment, and command, whereby we apply that judgment. [4] Prudence is the virtue that disposes practical reason to discern our true good in every circumstance and to choose the right means of achieving it.[5] It is an intellectual and moral virtue and refers to practical reason and not speculative reason. [6]

"A friend, and a prudent friend, can help to shape a friend's decision. He does so by virtue of that love which makes the friend's problem his own, the friend's ego his own.... For by virtue of that oneness which love can establish he is able to visualize the concrete situation calling for decision, visualize it, from, as it were, the actual center of responsibility... Such genuine and prudent loving friendship which has nothing in common with sentimental intimacy, and indeed is rather imperiled by such intimacy, is the sine qua non for genuine spiritual guidance." [7]

Mary had Prudence in saying Yes to her humble participation in salvation history.
But Mary treasured up all these things and pondered them in her heart. [8]

Wisdom sees into false situations and confronts if necessary.
For wisdom is a kindly spirit and will not free a blasphemer from the guilt of his words; because God is witness of his inmost feelings, and a true observer of his heart, and a hearer of his tongue. Because the Spirit

of the Lord has filled the world, and that which holds all things together
knows what is said; therefore no one who utters unrighteous things will
escape notice, and justice, when it punishes, will not pass him by. [9]

1   Wisdom 8:4, 5
2   STIIaIIae 47.2 ad 1
3   STIIaIIae 47.4
4   STIIaIIae47.8
5   CCC 1806
6   www.admethics.com
7   The Four Cardinal Virtues, Dr. Josef Pieper
8   Luke 2:19
9   Wisdom 1:6-8

My reflections.
Lectio, reading the Scripture...slowly

Meditation, drawn to these words...

Prayer of the heart...

Contemplation...silence

Justice

Who executes justice for the oppressed; who gives food to the hungry.
The LORD sets the prisoners free; the LORD opens the eyes of the blind.
The LORD lifts up those who are bowed down; the LORD loves the righteous. [1]

God is Justice and Mercy, and both demands were met through Jesus' sacrifice on the cross. Thomas Aquinas wrote, "Justice without mercy is cruelty. Mercy without justice is the mother of dissolution." A soul filled with the virtue of Justice possesses a great concern for the divine rights of others, complemented by the drive to do something about it. An intellect filled with Prudence knows what is right; a will filled with Justice chooses to act for the good of others. [2]

Aquinas wrote, "He who is not angry when there is just cause for anger is immoral. Why? Because anger looks to the good of justice. And if you can live amid injustice without anger, you are immoral as well as unjust." This does not condone violence or further sin, but passion to repair injustices. We pray for God's wisdom to act according to these ideas for the common good. He saw Justice as the second most important virtue and considered it "rendering to another his due by a perpetual constant will." It is concerned with the will, rights, and common good and gives to man that which he is owed. A person who acts unjustly creates an inequality within the community, a disturbance of the order by which all are members of the community are fundamentally equally ordered to the common good of the community as participants in it. [3]
Next you will understand righteousness and justice and equity, every good path; [4]

We ask for wisdom and revelation in resolving issues needing compassion and just changes. On punishment for injustice, Aquinas wrote: The punishments of this present life are more medicinal than retributive, for retribution is reserved for the divine judgment. [5]

1	Psalm 146:7, 8
2	ST II-II, 58, 1
3	ST II-II, q. 66, a. 6
4	Proverbs 2:9
5	ST II-II, q. 66, s. 6

My reflections.
Lectio, reading the Scripture...slowly

Meditation, drawn to these words...

Prayer of the heart...

Contemplation...silence

Fortitude

Be strong and of good courage, do not fear or be in dread of them;
for it is the Lord your God who goes with you; he will not fail you or forsake you. [1]

St. Teresa of Avila wrote, "To have courage for whatever comes in life—everything lies in that." Fortitude is the cardinal virtue of courage and strength to help us confront fear and uncertainty. Courage is a compulsion to go beyond our fears to trust God. *"Our Lord who sustains the world"* was the message Joan of Arc had painted on her battle flag. She was the most courageous saint of the Middle Ages as a leader and defender of France during war with England. At 19, she was given permission to restore Charles II as the King of France as she led the army. Joan was told in dreams at 13 that she would one day liberate France, and she encouraged the army, "Trust in God." She was finally defeated in Paris and burned at the stake in 1431 by the English who said after her death, "We are all lost for it is a good and holy woman that has been burned." [2]

St. Joan was canonized in 1920 and committed her life to unity along with St. Catherine of Siena of Italy. Pope Benedict wrote that St. Joan of Arc "fearlessly took the great light of the Gospel to the complex eras of history. She invites us to a lofty level of Christian life: to make prayer the guiding thread of our days; to have full confidence in fulfilling the will of God, whatever it is; to live in charity without favoritisms, without limits and having, in the love of Jesus, a profound love for the Church. We could place her next to the holy women who *stayed* on Calvary, close to Jesus crucified, and Mary, his mother, while the apostles fled and Peter himself denied him three times." [3]

If God is our true authority and has spoken on an issue he cares about, we are safe. Even as St. Joan of Arc was martyred, she was a joyful, strong woman who was married to Jesus, her beloved.

Whom have I in heaven but Thee? And there is nothing
upon earth that I desire besides thee. [4]

1   Deuteronomy 31:6
2   https://the-american-catholic.com Joan of Arc: Saint of Courage
3   Benedict XVI General Audience 26January2011. https://www.vatican.va/content/bennedict-xvi
4   Psalm 73:25

My reflections.
Lectio, reading the Scripture...slowly

Meditation, drawn to these words...

Prayer of the heart...

Contemplation...silence

Temperance

Every athlete exercises self-control in all things. They do it to receive a perishable wreath, but we an imperishable. [1]

St. Augustine advised, "Seek what suffices, seek what is enough, and don't desire more. Whatever goes beyond that produces anxiety, not relief." He was healed from a sex addiction by grace, scripture, prayer, sacraments, and help of his mentor, St. Ambrose.

St. Thomas Aquinas stated, "Temperance is simply a disposition of the mind which sets bounds to the passions." The Catechism states: Temperance is the moral virtue that moderates the attraction of pleasures and provides balance in the use of created goods. It ensures the will's mastery over instincts and keeps desires within the limits of what is honorable. [2]

St. John Chrysostom wrote, "The drunken man is a living corpse. Wine is given us of God, not that we might be drunken, but that we might be sober; that we might be glad, not that we get ourselves pain." About food, St. Alphonsus Liguori warned, "It is almost certain that excess in eating is the cause of almost all the diseases of the body, but its effects on the soul are even more disastrous." That is motivation and conviction!

St. Teresa of Avila said, "Our body has this defect that the more it is provided care and comforts, the more needs and desires it finds." I understand this to be true from my perpetual desire for frozen yogurt, any flavor, with nuts, even in winter! Our bodies are not designed to overly restrict *or* binge, so temperance is possible as we pray and understand the effects of sudden sugar consumption, avoidance of food groups, and the pain underlying eating disorders. Making healthy choices, choosing a joy movement exercise, and developing our gifts and talents are ways to manage weight and enjoy food without fear. We are also not designed to entrust others for our decisions on eating. Celebrating life involves food from all the food groups. Give us wisdom and strength, Lord, to enjoy your creation with temperance!

1   I Corinthians 9:25-27
2   CCC 1809

My reflections.
Lectio, reading the Scripture...slowly

Meditation, drawn to these words...

Prayer of the heart...

Contemplation...silence

Made in the USA
Middletown, DE
16 April 2022

64186780R00056